IT'S TIME TO EAT DARK CHOCOLATE

It's Time to Eat DARK CHOCOLATE

Walter the Educator

Silent King Books
A WhichHead Entertainment Imprint

Copyright © 2024 by Walter the Educator

All rights reserved. No part of this book may be reproduced in any manner whatsoever without written per- mission except in the case of brief quotations embodied in critical articles and reviews.

First Printing, 2024

Disclaimer

This book is a literary work; the story is not about specific persons, locations, situations, and/or circumstances unless mentioned in a historical context. Any resemblance to real persons, locations, situations, and/or circumstances is coincidental. This book is for entertainment and informational purposes only. The author and publisher offer this information without warranties expressed or implied. No matter the grounds, neither the author nor the publisher will be accountable for any losses, injuries, or other damages caused by the reader's use of this book. The use of this book acknowledges an understanding and acceptance of this disclaimer.

It's Time to Eat DARK CHOCOLATE is a collectible early learning book by Walter the Educator suitable for all ages belonging to Walter the Educator's Time to Eat Book Series. Collect more books at WaltertheEducator.com

USE THE EXTRA SPACE TO TAKE NOTES AND DOCUMENT YOUR MEMORIES

DARK CHOCOLATE

It's time for a snack, oh, what a delight!

It's Time to Eat

Dark
Chocolate

Dark chocolate's waiting, so yummy and right.

A square so smooth, rich, and sweet,

A tiny treasure we can't wait to eat!

The wrapper crinkles, the treat is near,

The smell of cocoa fills the air so clear.

A deep, bold flavor, a little bite,

Dark chocolate makes the moment bright.

Snap! Goes a piece, just one or two,

It melts on your tongue like magic glue.

Not too sugary, just the right blend,

A treat so lovely, it's like a friend!

"Where does it come from?" you might say,

From cocoa beans, far, far away.

They're grown on trees in the sun's warm glow,

Then turned into chocolate we all know.

It's Time to Eat

Dark Chocolate

Some like it plain, so rich and neat,

Others add nuts or fruit so sweet.

There's chocolate with mint, or orange zest,

But dark chocolate, oh, it's the best!

"It's kind of bitter," says little Sam,

"But I like it better than jelly or jam!"

Each taste is bold, a grown-up treat,

But kids love it too, it's hard to beat!

Chocolate gives energy, a boost so small,

Perfect for sharing with friends big and small.

It's a moment of joy, a simple surprise,

A gift of flavor for mouth and eyes.

But don't eat too much, just a square or two,

Dark chocolate's magic is best shared with you.

Take it slow, enjoy the taste,

It's Time to Eat

Dark Chocolate

No need to hurry, no need to waste.

With every bite, we smile so wide,

A little square fills us with pride.

Whether after lunch or as a treat at night,

Dark chocolate makes everything feel just right.

So when it's time for a snack so sweet,

Dark chocolate's the treat we love to eat.

A square of joy, rich and bold,

It's Time to Eat

Dark
Chocolate

A story of cocoa, forever told!

ABOUT THE CREATOR

Walter the Educator is one of the pseudonyms for Walter Anderson. Formally educated in Chemistry, Business, and Education, he is an educator, an author, a diverse entrepreneur, and he is the son of a disabled war veteran.
"Walter the Educator" shares his time between educating and creating. He holds interests and owns several creative projects that entertain, enlighten, enhance, and educate, hoping to inspire and motivate you. Follow, find new works, and stay up to date with Walter the Educator™

at WaltertheEducator.com

www.ingramcontent.com/pod-product-compliance
Lightning Source LLC
LaVergne TN
LVHW052011060526
838201LV00059B/3979